Principles

To Remember and Apply

Principles to Remember and Apply

Cover Designs by Maile — Typesetting by Fit To Print, Sedona, AZ

Printed in the United States of America
by Mission Possible Commercial Printing, Sedona, AZ

Published by Light Technology
P.O. Box 1526
Sedona, Arizona 86339
(602) 282-6523

Library of Congress Catalog Card Number

ISBN 0-929385-59-4

Acknowledgments

To the One Source of All-that-IS whose unfailing Presence and support made it all possible, unending love and gratitude.

To son Kevin and his wife Donna deep appreciation for the indefinite loan of the computer that greatly facilitated the joyous work of writing, assembling and editing the material.

To dear friends, Jeanne, Jewel and Veronica heartfelt thank-yous for somehow managing to fit into busy schedules the indispensable task of checking the manuscript.

To Brenda of Fit To Print, sincere appreciation for her patient, sensitive and skillful approach to the process of typesetting.

Principles . . .

Principles

To Remember and Apply

Principles . . .

Introduction

This book is to be read with the heart as well as the mind. It contains nothing new. It is based on material written in the small hours of the morning over many years. An internal feeling of validity suggested that it be shared. The book is intended to spark and expand your *own* remembrance.

Pervading the entire book and central to the material is the idea of God and Creation as *inseparably* One. The Universal Mind deep within the center of our BEing already knows everything that is *true.* This knowing is found in the inner stillness of a quiet mind. It is here that we connect with the Source of All-that-IS. Sadly, the active, surface mind of intellect forms a barrier to true knowing. We need to expand our awareness of the eternal principles and apply them *here and now.*

Principles . . .

About the format:

To avoid misinterpretation, word-symbols that relate to God and Creation begin with capital letters. The term "Heart-Mind" or "heart-mind," whichever is appropriate, is a contrivance to emphasize the idea of unity of the mind and emotion. It helps to consider them as equal partners.

A variety of interchangeable names and terms have been used. If you choose to substitute mentally other terms with which you are more familiar and comfortable, be sure the *meaning* of the text is not altered.

The charts on the following pages show in condensed form some of the principles on which the writing is based. There is an appendix offering affirmations and some sources for further reading and study.

Principles . . .

GOD

Everywhere, All Powerful, All Knowing, All Loving, Eternal

God-Creation — Some interchangeable terms

Father-Mother	Creator	GOD	Mind-Idea	Source	Spirit
Child of God	Creation	Universal Christ-Self	Thought	All-that-IS	Spirit

State of BEing experienced as:

Unity — Truth — Reality — God's World — Heaven — The Kingdom — Home

Life-Energy of God-Creation is "seen" as Universal Light and "felt" as Unconditional Love

The access to the Reality of God's World from the illusion of the material world is:

Christ Consciousness within

illusion of separateness from GOD

unreality — error

personal self — individuality

fear — guilt

space-time — form — density — physical body

perception of a five-sensory, three-dimensional world of duality

differences – analysis – judgment

Being concepts, the dualities are countless. Here are a few examples:

reality/unreality; truth/error; life/death; love/hate; light/darkness; peace/war; good/evil; health/sickness; strength/weakness; happiness/sorrow; gain/loss; and so on...

Principles . . .

Principles

To Remember and Apply

Principles . . .

GOD

GOD IS!

GOD is MIND

GOD is MIND and IDEA

GOD-MIND-IDEA create THOUGHT

GOD-MIND-IDEA-THOUGHT create LIFE-ENERGY

all is

ETERNALLY ONE!

In the "beginning" was/is the one creative Mind of God. The Thought of this Mind perpetually generates Life-Energy. Life-Energy is the expression of God and includes All-that-IS.

God comprises Creation. In the totality of Creation, God is all-inclusive. God and Creation are inseparable. This perfect, harmonious unity exists beyond any imagined illusion of a physical world. As spiritual BEing manifesting Life-Energy, we are always united with God, the Source of All. All is One.

Nothing can alter the reality and simplicity of God's World, our place in It and Its place in us. We can and do seem to experience countless worlds of illusion made with a complexity of thought systems having a multiplicity of effects.

Granted, God and Creation may *appear* to be obscured to a greater or lesser degree by misty veils, the dreams of illusion. At times God's World seems to come and go—-perhaps to be seen dimly or in bright bursts.

The joyous Truth is that God and Creation are still there, here and everywhere, unchanged and readily accessible. We must be *ready and willing* to let the heart-mind go beyond, or through, these mists of illusion that so distort our vision and experience. When we surrender totally to the God-Self that is always within us, these so-called barriers prove to be nothing.

God created a perfect World. This simple universal Truth can be called Reality. Humanity collectively and individually has accepted a false concept of an existence apart from God. We have chosen to perceive and manifest Creation imperfectly.

A desert mirage seems real. The rational mind knows that it is an effect of light refraction; but the senses say, "I see it! It must be real." Likewise, the outer world seems real because the senses confirm it. The world of form is an illusory trick of the human mind.

The appearance of forms we see with the physical eyes and the interactions of so-called individual life-expressions are the effects of a mistaken belief that disconnection from God is *possible*. The physical world and all it represents is the result of focusing on diversity rather than on universality.

The reversal, or correction, of the error of disunity must first be made by each of us individually. This means allowing ourselves, starting *where we seem to be*, to: recognize the underlying unity of Life-Energy; see the uniformity of Light that interpenetrates form; feel the unconditional Love and Peace that this recognition brings.

When a sufficient number of us transcend the illusion of separateness and imperfection, correction of these errors is made collectively. Then All Creation will be *consciously* manifesting Its perfection.

This is the undoing of the *idea* of separation from our Creative Source. This healing of the idea of a dual mind allows us to become aware that all is *One Mind, One Spirit, One Life* forever functioning peacefully without the limitation of space, time or form.

Space-Time and Form

Concepts of space, time and form do not exist in the Mind of God because Its Thought is universal and limitless. Electromagnetic Life-Energy exists everywhere, continually generated by Thought.

Space and time are perceived as the *apparent distance between points.* Space involves location, while time involves events. They are interlocked and can be called "space-time." It is unreal because each component depends on limited, variable perception.

The *idea* of space-time is an attempt by seemingly individual minds to see the Energy-flow in artificial segments. The *idea* of form is an attempt to condense Energy into shifting patterns of limited duration. Space and form are mutually definitive. These concepts comprise the background against which the drama or dreams of human existence seem to be played.

The human mind, seeing itself divorced from God, is preoccupied with the idea that life manifests as dense physical form in the context of space-time. It does not really see and is not truly aware of a unified *continuity* of existence without form, time or space.

Since All Creation is an inseparable part of the One Universal Mind whose Thought produces Life-Energy, all is collectively a composite sentient, or conscious, Energy field. This Energy field, or Spirit, that constitutes our true expression and that of everything everywhere is *unformed, unlimited and eternal.*

The ideas of space-time and form cannot exist without the idea of separateness. They depend upon the interpretation of observations and are relative to the physical location and mental focus of the perceiver. These factors show them to be illusions.

At this point you may be wondering what all this has to do with our functioning in this material world. We do seem to be caught up in the numberless false "realities" of the three-dimensional world and the five physical senses.

How do we deal with the messages of space-time and form given to us by these physical senses and the human mind? We remember that there is a *Reality* in which they do not exist. This requires an intense, heartfelt desire for *awareness* of the eternal Truth of Creation and total surrender to the guidance of the *internal* God-Self.

Ideas of space-time and form anchor mortal minds to dreams of a material world and set the stage for playing out dramas based on separateness, fear and guilt. In Truth "time" is eternity, complete and uninterrupted.

Eternity may be a difficult concept to grasp if we are convinced of the so-called reality of *linear* time: past, present and future. Even in a material world, the only aspect of time that we can actually relate to is *NOW*.

The present instant is the only element of time that offers us the opportunity to change our thoughts, feelings, beliefs and, therefore, our experience. In the present, we are able to exercise the faculty of choice; obviously we cannot do this in the past nor in the future.

Change of perception, relinquishment of judgment, fear and guilt can only be done *now*—in the present. *Now* is the only time we can extend Love, Peace and Joy. *Now* is the only time we can experience Life or anything at all. This means that the past can have no validity for us; nor can the future. In the *now* we are free to BE.

Now is the door to eternity; the opening into Light, Love, Peace and Joy; the condition of experience; a requisite of knowledge; the state of BEing. The "past" is an illusion and the "future" a fantasy. *Now* is where the healed state is found; it is an element of The Whole. The Kingdom of Reality is *now.*

All the so-called ills of mortality are only recollections of an unreal past and fears of a similar future. *Now* is the escape from both. *Now* cannot be experienced while the heart-mind is focused on memories of the past and anticipation of the future. *Now* is found in the stillness of mind, a cessation of thought, that allows BEingness to be recognized.

Surrender ideas of past and future to the Heart-Mind that knows only the eternal *now.* It is here that the I AM of All exists. Here is freedom from fear and guilt.

GOD'S

CREATION

IS

WITHOUT

ANY

l

i

m

i

t

s

Will and Law

In "The Lord's Prayer," Jesus refers to the *Will* of God. God's Will for all Creation is perfect, endless unity of Spirit. The continual replication of God in Creation is God's Will in action. Creation is a complete and totally unified spiritual clone of God!

God's Will is the *only* will. The human mind is concerned with what it sees as needs, wants and wishes. It interprets God's Will from the human or personal standpoint. It incorrectly assumes that the function of Will is to supply some *material* desire.

When we align our feelings and thoughts with God's Will, we know that as Spirit, whole and complete, we do not really *need* anything. So-called needs of the outer world are sometimes met as a result of being in tune with God's Will and acknowledging the perfection and order of every aspect of Creation.

Here in this world we can surrender to God's Will and choose the path lit by universal unconditional Love; or we can choose an unlit road under the domination of the mortal self. As always, which choice we make is apparent in its consequences.

It is possible at times to feel or think we are accepting God's Will when we are merely thinking we ought to or would *like* to make that choice. This ambivalence produces a vacillation between "high" and "low" states of mind. When we are firmly committed to surrendering the so-called "human will," vacillations or setbacks seldom occur because we are in harmony with the true Self – with God and total Creation.

The Will of God and the Law of God are linked. The Will is exercised eternally in continual Creation. The Law governs the condition in which the Will is expressed.

Life, Light, Love, Peace and Joy are provisions of God's Law. When any of these elements seem to be absent from our daily experience, we can be sure that we are not thinking in harmony with the universal Mind of God—the Christ-mind *within* us.

There is no Will or Law but that of the Mind of God, Source of all that is Real. Reality, or Truth, can only be experienced within the harmonious order of Will and Law, unhampered by concepts of and identification with individual human "minds" and dense forms. Thoughts and feelings that are not in harmony with God's Law are unreal and have no real meaning.

In the ISness of God we find our BEing, our *collective identity* as the One Child of God. We must be willing to release that which is not in accord with the Law and obscures the vision and experience of the true Self.

Man's "laws" might better be called *rules*. The material world does require rules to help handle the seeming chaos. In contrast to God's Law which is changeless and eternal, these rules are variable, numerous and conflicting. They depend upon geography, culture, history and expectations—in other words, the old familiar illusion of space-time and form.

The law of cause and effect operates in both God's Real World, or Heaven, and the dream world of illusion. In God's World, God is Cause and Creation is Effect. Since God and Creation are One, God is *both* Cause and Effect! In Heaven contrasts and conflicts are impossible.

In the material world, "good" (loving, kindly, peaceful, and so on) feelings and thoughts cause happy effects. "Bad" (unloving, unkind, vengeful and so forth) feelings and thoughts cause unhappy effects.

The law of cause and effect operates through the agency of Energy or Power. All Power is of God and, as said before, is an effect of Thought. Energy and Thought are a part of the creative Mind that produces them.

Power is both generated and used in the creative process. Thought, as producer and recipient of Power, when further energized by *feeling*, has the ability to bring into manifestation the ideas being thought about. The Power of either Divine or human thought must not be underestimated.

Individually and collectively, we have the capacity to use and direct this Power in harmony with the Mind of God on behalf of the holiness of All Creation. All effects in the realm of Spirit are harmonious, perfect, universal and luminous with the Light and Love of the Source of All-that-IS.

The human mind mistakenly thinking it is a separate entity has the capacity to *misuse and misdirect* the Power of God. This is how the law of cause and effect can seem to operate with apparently disastrous effects. In this situation we appear to be in a worldly environment that is fractured, chaotic, unloving, fearful and painful.

Such effects can be reversed both individually and collectively by a change of feelings, thoughts and beliefs. Correction of the idea of disunity starts with individual reversal of feeling and thought patterns. Collective correction follows.

We appear to have two choices in the way we use the Power of God; but is there *really* a valid alternative when the Source of All *IS ALL*? The choice for error is a non-choice—a choice for nothingness.

Duality

The concept of duality arises with the acceptance of the ideas that it is possible to divorce God from creation and that mind can be split. Again, in God's World (Heaven or Reality) all is One. The creative Mind of God is not split. There is only *one* Mind.

However, the human mind *sees itself as split.* There is a deep inner core of consciousness that *does* remember the Truth about the Real World. This is the Self, or universal Christ, within all Creation. The illusion of disunity cannot really hide the existence of this link with our Source.

The rational, active, surface part of the human mind is focused on the outer, material, sensory world and accepts it as "truth." This focus of the surface mind on the outer world of appearances *seems* to block awareness of the God-Self within.

Having accepted the error of disunity, the human mind extends it to encompass its entire thought system. This is the origin of the "dualities." They are symbolized in the Greek myth of Pandora's box and in the Biblical story of the fruit of the tree of knowledge of "good" and "evil" in the Garden of Eden.

The chart in the introductory pages lists some of the numerous concepts of duality. You can easily think of many others. Some people find it is helpful temporarily to make a list of them in two columns starting with:

unity —— disunity
love —— fear . . .

It is obvious that terms in the first column express *ideas* that are in harmony with, or a reflection of, God's Thought and that the others do not. Later the "disunity" column can be symbolically discarded .

It is assumed that the presence of fear-based concepts in the heart-mind is made clear by the obvious contrast to their love-oriented opposites. Let us look at a few examples of fear-related ideas:

Possession, greed and jealousy are closely linked. In each case, an individual person wants to have something else that is separate. Each expresses *fear of loss or lack.*

Ownership is in itself neither "wrong" nor "right." It is the desire or feeling of *need* to possess that requires correction.

Try substituting "the" for the possessive pronoun "my!" For instance, *the* house...*the* car...*the* pet...*the* wife or husband...*the* child...*the* bank account... Do you feel a difference?

In the case of greed, a person seen as "greedy" is fearful that he-she will be deprived of something that is thought to be needed or wanted. The person may already have everything that is needed but is fear-driven to accumulate more and more.

Jealousy entails fear of loss of a possession which is seen as valuable and is coveted by someone else. Also, jealousy may be based on resentment as well as fear when someone else possesses something that the "jealous" one seems to lack.

The presence of separateness, fear, loss and lack is unmistakable in the errors of possessiveness, greed and jealousy. The correction is: first, substitution of the idea of *oneness* for separateness; and second, application of the principle of *abundance*. God's Life-Energy is abundant and includes *universal Love.*

Anger, grievance, resentment and attack form another related fear-based group. Here is fear of injury to the personal self on a physical, emotional or mental level. As always, the element of separateness, or disunity, is clearly evident. There is the memory of past hurt and fear of repetition. Anger may be hidden or obvious.

Attack, often misunderstood, appears to take place between separate individuals and is a projection of anger outward. By believing attack is *possible* and seeing another as a *potential* attacker, the one playing a role of "victim" both attacks and invites attack!

Fear-laden thoughts and feelings involving anger, grievance, resentment and attack call for application of the principles of *oneness and trust.* There must be total *forgiveness* and unconditional *love* for each and every aspect of Creation.

The use of the words "positive" and "negative" to indicate good (truth) or evil (error) has been avoided. Life-Energy is an *idea* in the Mind of God. Its manifestation as *electromagnetic energy* is a continual, balanced interaction between electric (positive) and magnetic (negative) force. What seems to be in opposition is actually a composite *whole*. It is well known that the Chinese long ago became aware of this cosmic energy as the Yin-Yang principle.

Some *apparent* dualities are reciprocal and can be thought of as a unit. A few examples to consider are: cause and effect; giving and receiving; teaching and learning. We have touched upon cause and effect. Receiving is the effect of giving, and learning is an effect of teaching. A giver receives then gives. A teacher learns and teaches. The cycles go on and on: giving-receiving-giving——teaching-learning-teaching.

A less obvious and perhaps more difficult concept of seeming duality is that of "male" and "female." The illusion of differences is indeed apparent in the idea of sex because physical *bodies* have the appearance of being either masculine or feminine.

However, Spirit is indivisible, complete, and should be thought of as being *sexless.* The earth-mind may find it easier to accept the idea that there is a reciprocal relationship between the so-called masculine and feminine *elements* of the heart-mind.

All the qualities we associate with *both* sexes are present in the mind and emotions of *each "person."* One of the reasons we choose to incarnate in a male or female body within a specific social environment is to learn to balance and integrate both the masculine and feminine aspects of the heart-mind.

Let us not forget that duality occurs *only* in the *illusion* since God's World is totally unified. If you have made a list, everything in each column is linked in concept to its respective heading of “unity” or ”disunity.” Words listed in the disunity column represent erroneous ideas relating to a peculiar, distorted, upside-down thought system.

Fear and guilt are the fundamental result of the false idea that mind is separate from Mind. A mind that *feels* cut off from its Source will certainly feel fearful and experience guilt for what it sees as its part in the error of separation from the One Mind.

If we choose to have divisive feelings and thoughts of fear and guilt, we program the heart-mind to attract those inner and outer experiences that are not loving, peaceful and happy.

In this world the concept of duality, which cannot exist without the idea of differences, always calls for judgment. Judgment entails comparison. Comparison requires thoughts about two or more *separate* elements.

People, events, places and actions are compared on the basis of appearance or effect and judged to be larger or smaller, better or worse, beautiful or ugly, loving or hateful and so forth. This thought process anchors the mind firmly in the illusion, strengthening the veil that *seems* to obscure the Truth.

A valid use of judgment is to recognize the difference between reality and unreality. In the material world, the ideas that are based upon love, peace, happiness and truth can be considered "real" since they *reflect* the Truth of God's World.

To judge anyone or anything as less than spiritually perfect makes it impossible to see the holiness of the real Self shining within everything. Differences perceived and judged are always divisive and serve to perpetuate the illusion of duality.

We seem to have much confusion in this world because of our insistence on judging everything by its outer appearance. This illusory dream world of multiple belief systems and their countless apparent effects could not seem to exist without the thought of duality.

In a world of duality, individual and collective beliefs are built thought upon thought, experience after experience, and are reinforced by feelings. When only *spiritually* linked thoughts and feelings enter and remain in the heart-mind, a spiritually based belief system is established.

The importance of random thoughts tends to be overlooked. Without being noticed, they slip down into the subconscious mind where they play a part in shaping beliefs. We know our thoughts determine the nature of the illusion we experience.

Loving, peaceful, gentle and joyful thoughts gravitate to and augment the God-like thought already stored deep within memory. From this center of awareness, remembrance of our true *identity* as Spirit surfaces. To have happy and harmonious outer experiences that reflect God's World, or Heaven, our thoughts must be compatible with God's Thought.

However, when random thoughts are fear-and guilt-based, they too gravitate to similar thoughts in the subconscious. Their inharmonious, hateful and fearful effects become unhappily apparent in the outer world.

G

O

D

I

I A M T H A T

S

O

N

E

Relationships

In Heaven, there is only *one* Relationship, that of God and Creation, changeless and eternal. The error of a fractured creation opens the door to experiencing many relationships here on earth.

Here, relationships revolve around the idea of role playing. Before taking on an infant body to have an earth experience, an entity chooses the major role to be assumed and the family relationships involved. Within that larger framework, many minor roles are adopted throughout the period of embodiment.

Shakespeare knew this well as is evidenced in the often quoted speech from "As You Like It":

> *"All the world's a stage:*
> *And all the men and women merely players;*
> *They have their exits and their entrances;*
> *And one man in his time plays many parts"*

Expanding on the metaphor of life here as a drama: we choose not only the role(s), we choose the period in which the drama is set; the scenery (where we are born or live); the costumes (clothing appropriate to the time and culture); the director (the God-Self or the human self). *The script is written by us from minute to minute, day by day, year after year as we interact with others.*

Roles are chosen to offer maximum opportunity for mental and emotional healing as well as overall spiritual awareness. When those who are playing roles on the earth plane interact with one another, a temporal relationship of short or long duration is formed.

Relationships offer wonderful opportunities to express universal, unconditional love and forgiveness. This is done by the perception of another as the spiritual Self— the holy Child of God perfectly created.

However, to be universal and unconditional, love must be all-inclusive. No one and no thing can be excluded, including what we think of as the self-Self. The extension of unconditional love is an affirmation of the unity of All Creation. It is a recognition that God's Creation is inseparable. It affirms the eternal linkage of Light, Peace and Joy to Divine Love.

Here on earth, the only role that we can play to perfection is that of the Holy Child of God which we *ARE*. All other roles seem to be affected by the unreliable dualities. We then become entangled in love-hate relationships.

In love-hate relationships, happiness and pain, trust and fear swing inconsistently back and forth in the heart-mind, clouding relationships that should be bright with love.

A love-hate relationship is specialized and depends on the idea of separateness for its apparent existence. It involves different "selves" judged to be separate from and outside the One Self within.

The basic "weapon" of a love-hate relationship is using someone or something else as a target for feelings and thoughts that are erroneous. It is more acceptable to the self to see its mistakes in others than to seek correction for its own error. This shifts blame for fear, guilt and grievances to someone else.

True forgiveness does not blame. It offers healing to the heart-mind caught in a love-hate relationship. Forgiveness overlooks fear and guilt, seeing no error. It removes the *ideas* of fear and guilt that seem to block unconditional love. It transforms a love-hate relationship into one that is healed.

Forgiveness is the immediate and complete healing of unloving, unpeaceful, judgmental thoughts and feelings. Judgment entails analysis and acceptance of a fractured world of appearances based on the erroneous concept of the duality of "good" and "evil."

Many people believe they are extending forgiveness when they think or say, "You have hurt me, but I forgive you." This does *not* constitute forgiveness. The human senses and mind do perceive hurt. The truly forgiving heart-mind does not accept the *idea* of harm as spiritually possible because it is not a concept in the Mind of God.

Forgiveness is needed in a world of illusion. It is not needed in God's perfect World. True forgiveness does not recognize error of any kind. It looks beyond appearances to the purity of Creation.

In this world there seems to be a tendency when considering the idea of adult relationships to think first of close family ties: spouse or partner; parent(s); sibling(s). It should be remembered that interaction with *any* aspect of Creation on any mental, emotional or physical level constitutes a relationship.

To "love" because the beloved is pleasing is merely a form of self-gratification, quickly reversed when the love-object becomes less pleasing. This pattern applies to relationships with all people and all things.

Here in the drama of illusion disappointment is likely if either partner enters into a relationship for the purpose of getting something from the other that he-she sees as missing in the self. This situation appears to offer love and happiness until that particular something sought is withdrawn by the other.

A role player can also enter into a relationship to disguise his-her insecurity by supplying to another something that seems to be lacking. A person tries to add to his-her self-importance by lessening that of the other. This impossible attempt frustrates the player. Spirit is not subject to comparison and has no lack.

The roles of the human personality frequently switch back and forth from one to another. This instability is characteristic of the world of illusion.

Whatever role is being played, the player needs to recognize and focus on the *spiritual* BEing—the Child of God—the One Self—in others. We are intended to reach beyond the specialness of personal relationships and universalize our loving feelings and thoughts. This means expanding love given to the few to include *All*, without distinction.

We are here in this three-dimensional world to learn to play the "game" of role playing by Universal rules, God's Law, rather than by the cultural rules of society. When cultural rules conflict with God's Law, there should be no question about which to obey.

When we have learned to play our roles by God's Law exclusively, we can be freed from the necessity of game playing and role assumption. When we *function* as the perfect Idea of our Source, we experience Life joyfully in Love and Light as we are created to do. This is release from the "karmic wheel."

God's Law is not something new to learn. It is something known that needs to be remembered and applied. To experience and extend unconditional love in a relationship with any aspect of Creation, the *heart* as well as the mind must be wide open and receptive.

It is appropriate to have *compassion* for those whose role playing blinds them to the awareness of their true nature and perfection. However, this compassion must take the form of loving recognition of the holy Child of God, the BEing of Light, within every partner in a relationship, without exception.

It is inappropriate to direct *sympathy* toward anyone playing a troublesome or painful role in a relationship. Sympathy focuses mental and emotional energy upon the so-called "problem" involved.

This misdirection of the Power of united feeling and thought reinforces the error. It makes the correction and release of the problem seem more difficult. The heart-mind of the sympathizer becomes clouded by the feelings and thoughts of the one toward whom the sympathy is directed.

Here on earth, the idea of sex is usually related to the physical body, its form and its so-called "needs." Relationships are often formed on the basis of sex. Balance, equality and reciprocity are important elements of harmony in a relationship.

A balanced relationship requires first that each partner recognizes and accepts equally his-her own masculine and feminine aspects. This gives each one the freedom to acknowledge and accept the balance of *both* of these aspects in the other.

The idea of integration of the male and female in the heart-mind fosters wholeness in a relationship. It is an important step in remembering and accepting unity with God. Eventually, all relationships will evolve to the point that brother-sisters acknowledge the presence of the sexless Child of God within ALL.

Let us not overlook the relationship with one's Self! There is a prevalent human tendency to do so. Honor and unconditional love are due to the internal God-Self that knows Its own perfection as an inseparable part of God and Creation. This Self extends the Power of God's Love and Light, gently and patiently from the vantage point of eternity.

Let this Holy Self, or Holy Spirit, be in charge; actively seek Its guidance. Be kind to and gentle with the little "self" that wanders through illusion while learning to let the seeming split from the One Self be healed.

If the human self lapses, do not judge and condemn it, nor hold grudge and grievance against it. This invites guilt that makes correction seem more remote. Instead, offer it unlimited love and total forgiveness. Remind this self of its Source.

In this world, an interesting and sometimes challenging relationship is that between children and parents or teachers. For one thing, it presents another example of the role playing by which the mortal mind maintains the illusion of disunity.

Children are not a special species because their bodies at first are very small and ability to use them develops relatively slowly. Spirit, the Life-Energy vitalizing the body, is ageless. It was whole before incarnation and remains so during apparent physical changes.

The spiritual "child" being the holy image of God is perfect. Parents make only the physical body. The part of a child's mind recognized as "personality" must cope with the environment of the *outer* world. At the same time, the child must be helped to grow in remembrance and awareness of the *inner* Self.

If the idea of reincarnation (another aspect of the illusion) is considered, children need wise and gentle guidance to help them re-orient to the appearances of a much changed outer world.

In infancy children often recognize the former roles of family members. Details of the previous earth plane existence may or may not be accessible in memory. If they remember, they may be unable to communicate the knowledge verbally. Of course, the illusion of in-between, discarnate intervals may be remembered by infants as well.

Parental responsibility is to love the Child of God within and to provide the best spiritual and physical environment of which the parent is capable. The rest is up to the child itself and is a part of the growth process which motivated incarnation.

A child reared in a spiritually-focused home will find the path of inner and outer growth much easier. The child is loved without taint of possession, pride or prejudice because it is God's creation.

When a parent or teacher focuses on the spiritual nature of a child, there will be less temptation to judge the *child* for seeming errors. This allows correction of mistakes rather than misperception of the child. Parents and teachers can gently and lovingly point out the path of wisdom and Truth.

If the child chooses to reject this help, the laws of cause and effect (karma) will operate in the child's instruction without parental involvement in a *harsh form of correction.* Children often learn a great deal more from adult actions, attitudes and feelings than they do from the spoken word.

Children's choices will attract the lessons that they need to learn. Some corrections we attempt to make in children's behavior stem from a self-oriented desire to have them fit a mold of our personal choosing. We can project what may or may not be perceived as our own faults or lacks upon children. We see a need for correction in them rather than in ourselves.

If we make rules for children that are not in harmony with the principles of God's Thought, it is not reasonable to expect the children to obey them! It may well be that a child incarnated for the express purpose of reversing some of these same man-made rules that we are trying to enforce.

The task of parents and teachers is to help children to see themselves, the world without and the world within reflecting the holy Light of God.

To teach children about Love, we must be loving; to teach Peace, we must be at peace with ourselves and others. Children are naturally joyful. This capacity can be sustained and increased by parents and teachers who are essentially happy. If we are to teach Truth, we must be consistently truthful with children.

Let us remind children of their true origin—their loving, peaceful nature as the Child of God who is One with All Creation. This practice should be started early in infancy while they are still close to the remembrance of God's World.

We are to see in children the perfection of Spirit and know that they have, in Truth, not changed since they were created as an *idea* in the Heart-Mind of God. We can also know that they mirror our own perfection since *all* is an inseparable part of the One Divine BEing.

Health

Here, health (wholeness) is natural and *reflects* the eternal principle of the perfection (Holiness) of God. Perfect health is the birthright of the One totally unified Child of God. Spirit is whole. All Creation is the spiritual manifestation of the Creator.

We need to allow the *idea* of health, or wholeness, that is already ours to fill the heart-mind. Light, Love, Peace and Joy are always found in the healed state of the heart-mind that knows and experiences its Oneness with God-Creation.

Healing is the *process* of restoring awareness of health to the heart-mind that has accepted the idea of disunity. There is no concept of this process in the Mind of God where only unity exists. In the total Oneness of God, All-That-IS functions perfectly. *There is nothing to heal.*

In this world, healing *is* necessary. Health must be restored to the heart-mind that has accepted the concept of illness of mind, emotion or body. It is important to remember constantly that severance from God and Creation is truly *impossible*. Since God is everywhere, all-powerful, all-knowing and eternal, it is obvious that the *idea* of separateness must be false.

It has been said repeatedly that healing this error entails eliminating thoughts and feelings of disunity, fear, guilt and related concepts from the consciousness. This can be done by surrendering them to the internal guidance of the spiritual Self, the universal Christ within.

Healing always starts with this complete change of feelings and thoughts; physical healing may follow. A belief system that accepts the idea of health of mind, emotion and body is essential for experiencing health.

There is a persistent tendency of the human mind to *identify* with the dense physical body, the symbol of separateness. Much emphasis is placed on the body's appearance, function and health.

The body is often considered to be the primary target for healing. When this happens, the role of feelings and thoughts is sometimes overlooked. Preoccupation with the apparent condition of the physical body can invite malfunction and be an obstacle to healing.

On earth, how a body is seen depends on the perception of the viewer. The flesh body seen with the physical eyes is not the only "body." Another level of perception reveals a less dense energy body. This body is the pattern for the physical body. Interwoven through all and connecting all is the eternal, universal Life-Energy of our Source.

The etheric body is affected by the input and outflow of thoughts and feelings. It absorbs and reflects loving, peaceful and joyful feeling-and-thought vibrations. The physical body responds by functioning in perfect harmony or health.

When the heart-mind has feelings and thoughts that are unloving, fearful and inharmonious, the etheric body seems to be adversely affected. This may cause unwanted changes in the physical body. It may take considerable "time" for the body to manifest an inharmonious pattern of ill health.

Illness has sometimes been plaintively protested because no immediate cause can be discerned; present thoughts and feelings seem blameless. It is not realized that the apparent cause may have occurred in the "past" and that physical changes were made slowly.

God's Thought is *collective* in the sense that It is totally unified. Like God, It is everywhere. It is available anywhere, anytime under any conditions. We need only to be willing, open and earnestly desire to receive It.

Thoughts and emotions sent forth by seemingly individual human minds have magnetic attraction. Those with similar vibrational content collect and accumulate in mass and effect. This is glorious if they are loving, joyous and in harmony with the Mind of God.

However; thoughts and feelings that are fearful, unloving and inharmonious reinforce the idea of disunity and its related concepts in the *collective human* consciousness. These must be screened *before* they drift into the "individual" subconscious mind where they are accepted *as if they were valid.*

God is manifested everywhere in the formless basic energy components of all Life. Every subatomic particle throughout an endless Universe of universes is created, energized and re-created by the Power of Mind. Every particle is sentient and perfect.

Here, so-called allergic reaction is an example of the effect of unhealthy thoughts accepted by human mind. Since the *concept* of illness is untrue, there is truly no validity to the idea of being adversely affected.

The "forms" we see are the result of the false ideas of disunity and duality. Misdirected human thought judges one form of substance to be beneficial and another to be harmful. Adverse reactions of mind, emotion and body are the result of accepting fearful thoughts and feelings that originate in the individual and collective heart-mind.

The physical body may receive confusing instructions that contradict the principles of *wholeness* and *perfection.* This confusion results in an imbalance of function and the appearance of unhealthy symptoms. Even in the illusion *none of this needs to be* when we remember the Truth of God's Creation.

Illness of mind, emotion and body is an apparent effect of a cause based on "past" illusion. If sickness is considered even to be *possible,* fear-laden thoughts and emotions can appear to be brought forward to manifest as disease.

An erroneous belief in imperfection renders the heart-mind and body vulnerable to that which is *feared.* Loving, peaceful, joyful and light-filled feelings and thoughts are keys to health of mind, emotion and body.

The apparent existence of the physical body as we know it is a result of the human mind's desire to *express* its belief in individuality. This erroneous idea causes hidden feelings of guilt that are uncomfortable even if the source of the discomfort is not recognized.

The physical body is neither a friend nor an enemy. It can be used as an instrument for health and peace or as a weapon. It is this dual possibility for use, either by the rational human mind or by Spirit, that demonstrates the neutrality of the body.

When the heart-mind is guided by the internal Christ-Self, or Spirit, the body is used to express wholeness and harmony on behalf of God's Truth. It can be perceived as a weapon when used under the direction of a mind that chooses to focus on the world's fear-filled dramas and role playing.

Healing requires that the heart-mind be focused on health and not on the problem. Whatever the cause and effect seem to be, the timeless principles of *wholeness* and *perfection now*, applied through the help of Spirit, brings healing to thoughts, feelings and ultimately to the body.

When spiritual healing is sought for an apparent physical malfunction, it is not helpful to analyze either the appearance or sensation of the symptoms. A name tag placed upon the seeming error tends to accord it a false feeling of validity. This focus of energy upon a problem reinforces and maintains it.

Acceptance as well as recognition of the fundamental principle of the *perfection* of God's Creation is necessary. This helps clear the heart-mind of any thoughts and feelings about the seeming difficulty.

Total concentration upon and silent surrender to the Power of the God-Self, or Spirit, *within* is required to neutralize the thought system responsible for the apparent malfunction. This process by-passes the superficial, rational, human mind.

The principles of spiritual healing can be applied not only to one's "own self," but to anyone and anything, anywhere. This is done *mentally* as an unspecific, universal exercise. Healing of mind and body through application of the principle of *perfection* blesses both the healed and the healer.

This does *not* mean that unrequested manipulative attempts should be made to change the apparent outer effects of another's thoughts. Each and every one is responsible for the chosen thoughts and feelings in the so-called individual human consciousness.

Error of any kind cannot be seen in others unless a concept of the error is also found in the *mind* of the observer. When this occurs, the one who would undertake healing someone else also needs healing. The focus of the heart-mind of the "healer" needs to be re-directed under the guidance of the One Mind.

Healing, like forgiveness, must be total. Health is wholeness, completeness. Unshakable *faith* in the Reality and Power of the Mind of God brings realization that in Truth there *is* nothing to be healed.

Transcending all physical appearances, there must be a certainty that *only* God and Creation are Real and that the perfection of Creation is not subject to change. This brings about the understanding and belief that God's World, a perfect Creation, can be *mirrored here* on earth.

Spontaneous healing of mind, emotion and body is a manifestation of the true relationship between the Created and the Creator. This idea may be difficult to understand because the collective human mind has *accepted* the mistaken idea of separateness from God. When there is *total* awareness of universality, the Oneness of all Creation with its Source, the healed condition is certain.

Acceptance of the idea of *timelessness* is necessary to understand the process of instantaneous healing. All the physical steps that would usually take days, weeks or months occur simultaneously. Each minute cell is restored to its perfect condition and function. It interacts in complete harmony with all other cells. Such a speed-up of physical processes conflicts greatly with the human mind's concept of time but is in perfect agreement with timelessness.

It has been said that in spiritual healing *total* surrender to the healing Power of the God-Self within is absolutely necessary. When this seems difficult, it may be well to seek help on the physical level where the so-called problem is seen.

If this course of action is chosen, it should still be remembered that *all* healing is of God. There has merely been a transferal of faith from a *direct* link to God to faith in a link with an agency (medical, herbal, chiropractic and so on) through which the Mind of God is seen to operate.

Healing of disharmony on a mental, emotional or physical level occurs when the heart-mind is brought into harmony with the Heart-Mind of God. Since Peace and unconditional Love are inseparable, it could be said that Love is the healer.

Aspects of healing that must never be overlooked are the principles of *praise* and *gratitude.* Praise and gratitude go hand in hand. They are the appropriate response to the *idea* that God created a perfect World. We feel thankful because, as Spirit, we and everything that exists are a unified part of that perfect World. We appreciate the truth that God is the Source of All and that All is One Life-Energy.

Praise of God recognizes the principle of *perfection* and attunes the human mind to the Source Mind. The perfection of God and Creation is sincerely, lovingly and joyfully praised, and we are thankful.

Praise and gratitude are due because it is known that the healed state, or wholeness, of All-that-Is *already exists* in the Mind of God. We have only to allow this principle to permeate the heart-mind.

Healing is the restoration of the principle of *truth* in a heart-mind that has accepted the mirage of the three-dimensional, five-sensory world as if it *were* real. Truth dissolves and releases meaningless memories of past fears, hates, conflicts and sorrows.

Willingness to let the past go is necessary for healing. Health always exists as an idea in the realm of Truth. However, it is not seen, manifested here in the outer world, without this vital *willingness* to give up the erroneous past.

The healed heart-mind is free to experience Light, Love, Peace and Joy *now*. It no longer seems split; it is whole—unified. A transformed heart-mind can transform the physical body. However, application of the principle of *health* must not be limited to the narrow interpretation of illness of the physical body.

Discussion of healing the physical body, emotions and mind leads inevitably to *ideas* of "life" and "death." The idea of death does not exist in the Mind that created an eternal World. How could death be real in a World where God's Life-Energy is always everywhere?

On the earth plane, a level of illusion that humanity seems to experience here, the dense physical body is almost always seen to be discarded eventually. In the material world of space-time, energy appears to leave a physical body "permanently." At varying rates of disintegration body-substance is released.

When there is no apparent evidence of life, the human mind tends to think that *Life* is gone. Not so! Loss of the dense form and appearance of the physical body *does not constitute loss of Life!* This validates the idea that there is no death.

The process is seen as "death" because of the human tendency to *identify with the physical body* instead of with Spirit. On another level of perception, still within illusion, Spirit and the lighter bodies continue to function fully. Life is not interrupted. Immortal Spirit is unaffected; It cannot "die."

The mere process of discarding the body and moving into another plane of existence does not automatically purify the human heart-mind! Lessons unlearned at the time of the transition must still be learned.

Life here can be considered as a school where we learn to remember and love God—to remember and *apply* spiritual principles. If the lessons are not learned here and now, it seems obvious that there must be the illusion of another earth experience—or a succession of them—until the lessons *are* learned.

Earlier it was said that the dense physical body is *almost always* discarded. There is another process that at present is unfortunately rare. It may become apparent that the necessary purification has been accomplished on the earth plane and transition to another plane of existence is appropriate. If identification is made *wholly* with Spirit, the universal Christ-Mind, or God-Self within, can release the thought-energy that holds the body particles (substance) in dense form so that the form *dissipates*.

By thought, the body can then also be re-formed in a lighter, more fluid condition to be used as needed. It is likely that this process was employed by the Christ Jesus in his resurrection and by other Masters who are reported to be able to “come and go” at will. All humanity is expected to evolve to the point where this is the *usual* method of transition!

Meditation

Since *Spirit*, not the physical body, is our real identity, how do we develop the awareness of this Truth? We know it is essential to focus the heart-mind only on love-related concepts. Our Oneness with God and All Creation must be constantly remembered. *However, this alone is not enough.*

"Be still and know that I AM God" (Psalms 46:10) is a biblical injunction—a signpost pointing to *The Way.* Most spiritual disciplines refer to stillness as being indispensable to the spiritual *awareness* of God manifested within All.

What is meant is the stilling of the active, rational, surface mind of the little "self". Daily meditation is a means whereby this stillness is achieved. *Meditation* is not to be confused with *contemplation* which engages the mind in thought!

There are several methods used in the practice of meditation. Whatever procedure proves the most helpful in reaching God in the quiet center of awareness within is the one to follow.

In the appendix, after the affirmations, are directions for the reader who is not familiar with the practice of meditation. While it is not necessary, some people find meditating to *soft instrumental* music helpful. A few of the many suitable available cassette tapes are listed.

Affirmative prayer is an essential preface to meditation. True prayer is not a supplication but an affirmation that God, as Source of All-that IS, has already provided everything that is *real.* There is nothing to ask *from* God. We offer heartfelt praise and gratitude *to* God for that which is *already given.* We seek and find increased communion with God.

The meditation directions given in the appendix suggest that one visualize and affirm being in and surrounded by a most brilliant white light. This is the *inner* Light that envelopes all people and things. It is important to do this both *before* and *after* meditating.

Beginners might do well to limit the daily periods of silent meditation to five or ten minutes each twice a day—-even less if it is necessary for any reason. The time can then be increased gradually. It can also be beneficial to participate in a silent meditation group once a week.

Experienced, consistent meditators probably are comfortable and happy spending twenty minutes upon waking in the morning and thirty or forty minutes prior to retiring at night. This devotes up to one hour a day set aside for *silent communion* with God.

It may be wise to spend no more than forty minutes in meditation at one sitting. The depth and intensity of *surrender to the silence* is more important than the duration of "time."

An instant or two of *total* surrender to the internal God-Self can be rewarding. If the rational, surface mind is slow to subside into silence, it may take longer to reach the inner level where a holy communion is experienced! Do not try to force meditation. If the time is not "right," try again.

It is a mistake to think that nothing is happening if "visions" are not seen nor "voices" heard. Although these phenomena do sometimes occur, they are not necessary for the *effectiveness* of meditation. The objective is deep and pervading peace, increase in the vibratory rate and a *feeling* of spiritual identity.

Consistent attention to and application of the Love-related healing principles, reinforced by daily prayer and meditation, can eventually lead to *vision* or expand it. The faculty of seeing is multi-level and multi-dimensional.

The word "vision" has several meanings. There is inner and outer vision. Both inner and outer seeing can relate either to sight or to the comprehension of ideas. Ideas can be either concrete (pertaining to space-time and form) or abstract (pertaining to feelings and thoughts).

Outer vision simply means seeing with the body's eyes. They send messages about the material world of space-time and form to the brain. Interpretation is made by this biocomputer in accordance with thoughts and emotions programmed by the past.

It is *inner vision* that is spiritually important to us. Visually this refers to *seeing* with the "mind's eye." This aspect of inner vision involves the pineal gland (often referred to as the third eye or the sixth chakra). This is how it is possible actually to *see Light,* the evidence of Life-Energy—the Reality of everything.

The communication aspect of inner vision is often spoken of as "insight." It is understanding given by the God-Self, the Christ Spirit within. It may take the form of internal hearing or of quiet, *wordless knowing.*

Inner knowing, or communication, does not necessarily occur *during* formal meditation and is not restricted to it. It can happen at *any* time when the active, rational outer mind is still—perhaps after meditating or even upon waking from sleep. Remember that meditation is the experience of a quiet but *alert* mind.

The *mystical* experience, or *revelation*, reveals spiritual information, or Truth, by means of inner vision, hearing and/or knowing. The *spiritual* content of a message will determine its validity.

The *psychic* experience utilizes the same faculties, but the messages usually relate to matters of the worlds of illusion. They may not always be accurate because illusion is variable and untrustworthy. It is impossible to know anything about the changeable temporal world—except that it *is* an illusion.

Meditation increases the receptivity of Energy (Power). Be not afraid of this Energy. Remember that *all* Power is of God. Let a forgiving heart-mind use It with *wisdom* and *gentleness.* God's Kingdom of Peace within overflows with the Power of Love and the Glory of Light about which Jesus spoke in his "Lord's Prayer."

*"A Course in Miracles" in Workbook Lesson 189, ***"I feel the Love of God within me now,"*** gives beautiful directions for meditation, although the word "meditation" is not used. It says in part:

"Simply do this: Be still and lay aside all thoughts of what you are and what God is; all concepts you have learned about the world; all images you hold about yourself. Empty your mind of everything it thinks is either true or false, good or bad, of every thought it judges worthy, and all the ideas of which it is ashamed. Hold onto nothing. Do not bring with you one thought the past has taught, nor one belief you ever learned from anything. Forget this world, forget this course, and come with wholly empty hands unto your God."

Summary

Repeated emphasis upon the reality of the total unity and perfection of God's Creation is necessary. The pervasive idea of division and imperfection in the appearances of this five-sensory, three-dimensional world needs constant correction.

It has been stressed that in the Reality of God's World, the Kingdom of Peace, correction of any kind is totally unnecessary. How can God"s universal principles of *perfection* and *completeness* be improved?

In this world, the basic principle of *correction* or *atonement*, as it is sometimes called, is of prime importance. Atonement in this sense is not to be interpreted as *punishment.* It involves only the correction and complete reversal of a distorted human thought system that believes separation from God and Creation is possible.

Identification with the dense physical body has been seen to be a factor that impedes recognition of the spiritual Self. This does not mean that the body is "evil." It has been pointed out that the body is neither holy nor unholy. It has been shown that it is the way it is *perceived* by the heart-mind that determines how it is used.

The body is an instrument that allows participation in the schooling provided by the various forms of illusion found here on earth. It deserves respect and reasonable care to enable it to function at its maximum potential and to fulfill its purpose.

However, it must be remembered that the body, its form and its appearance are not *you.* It must never be forgotten that *you are a spiritual BEing who is temporarily using a physical body.*

Because All Creation is an *idea* in the Mind of God, a unified expression of Life-Energy, we know that the only identification truly possible is with Spirit, the universal Christ within all things. Reality or Heaven is the Home of everything that IS.

On earth, the experience of love, peace and happiness depends on placing all thoughts and feelings under the loving guidance of the Christ-mind deep within consciousness. Forgiveness and unconditional love are extended to *every* brother-sister and to *all* things.

Here in the illusion of unreality, we cannot think or say that we love God if we do not have unconditional love for All Creation. To love the all-inclusive One Self, One Child, unconditionally *is* to love God. We cannot see, know or love the Creator if love is withdrawn from *any* part of Creation.

Fearful thoughts and feelings neither recognize nor accept the holiness of the One Child of God, the One Creation, in everyone and everything. Recognition and acceptance of this fact are necessary for healing the mind, emotions and body.

In Truth, *Principle* is the *idea* of holiness, or wholeness. It is the perfection of the Oneness of God and Creation, of universal Life-Energy, Light and Love. In this material world of seeming density and limitation, the spiritual principles that correct the error of disunity *reflect* this Principle.

When attention is directed to the appearance of imperfection, the heart-mind is not focused on Spirit. When unconditional love is not being expressed in *all* relationships, the illusion of severance from God and Creation is not only experienced but reinforced.

It is clear that the principle of *Truth* is the opposite of illusion and that the principle of *Oneness* is the opposite of separateness. Truth or Reality, Oneness or Unity, Light, Love, Joy and Peace are *conditions* in the state known as Heaven or God's Real World.

Life-Energy, Light, Love, Joy and Peace are how Reality and Unity are *expressed*. All are inseparable *ideas*. These spiritual principles are God-oriented ideas to be accepted in the human thought-and-belief system.

These principles can and should be applied to all situations that seem to arise in the material world. They bridge the gap between Truth and illusion. They reinforce chosen love-based, non-judgmental attributes such as trust, forgiveness, gentleness, kindness, patience, honesty, humility and consistency. They lead surely to complete awareness of Oneness.

In this material world it is vital to choose to acquire and express these love-based, non-judgmental qualities:

Trust implies perfect faith in and surrender to the Power of God that is shared by all Creation. It entails willingness to let go of false ideas accepted as "real" by a seemingly separate human self, the individual personality.

Forgiveness simply means focusing on and seeing only the perfection of every aspect of God's Creation without reservation. It means awareness that there is nothing to forgive.

Gentleness and *kindness* are often mistakenly confused with human weakness. The strength and fearlessness of complete trust and forgiveness are required to be truly gentle and kind in thought, feeling and action.

Patience is based on trust and gentleness. Moreover, it recognizes the unreliability of "time." It accepts the implication of eternity and the harmonious interaction of all Creation.

Honesty calls for scrupulous adherence to truth in relationships with others and with the self. Total honesty requires remembrance of the truth of our Oneness with All-that-IS. Honesty recognizes our identity as Spirit. It is dishonest to think any aspect of Creation is separate and imperfect.

Humility remembers and is thankful for the perfection of God's Creation. It is inappropriate to use the term to convey an idea of inadequacy or incompleteness.

Consistency requires unshakable trust and constant awareness of love-based attributes in the heart-mind.

In the Real World of God, Truth needs no recognition; it simply *IS*. In this material world how is reality, or truth, recognized by a heart-mind that is temporarily engaged in feelings and thoughts relating to the illusion of disunity and duality?

There must be a *sincere desire* and *willingness* to let go of unreal, divisive fear-based thoughts and feelings. This makes possible complete surrender of the heart-mind to the guidance of Spirit, the Christ-Self within. Now, the Thought of this Self can penetrate the receptive heart-mind and correct the erroneous fear-and-guilt-ridden thoughts and feelings.

Reality, or Unity, and Its expression as Light, Love, Joy and Peace can never be eliminated or even threatened. However, complete receptivity is required to experience their reflection here.

Spirit, or the God-Self, is the part of our mind that has not changed since Creation. It never accepted the idea of severance from the Mind of God.

When we begin to identify with Spirit, the little spark of Light always present within begins to expand. It illumines the inseparable, universal Love, Joy and Peace that await being recognized and experienced.

Love can be known by a feeling of radiance and connectedness to All-that-IS. This recognition is a result of the release of fearful thoughts and feelings. Love is accompanied by its companion Joy.

Finally, an unmistakable awareness of Peace floods the entire heart-mind. The combined, all-inclusive presence of Light, Love, Peace and Joy in the heart-mind is *evidence* of Truth, or Reality.

Often in this world the human mind's interpretation of peace is merely a temporary cessation of war. No matter how prolonged, the period of truce between confrontations and wars is *not* the genuine peace of mind that reflects the eternal Peace of God.

We cannot think, talk or write about peace and brother-sisterhood if any part of Creation is rejected, unappreciated and unloved. War in any form is *not* holy. So long as the heart-mind seems split, so long as it is involved with fear-based differences, comparisons and judgments, true peace is not being experienced.

In order to have a lasting peace that expresses God's Peace here and *now* in this world, each person, each nation and collective humanity must *feel* the undivided nature of God and Creation. All must be loved unconditionally and joyfully.

Summary

This book is primarily about the remembrance of Truth and Its application to correct the effect of illusions *here* where we appear to function in dense physical bodies. Other levels of experience may unfold as spiritual awareness progresses.

Jesus said, **"In my Father's house are many mansions..."** (St. John 14:2). Metaphysicians and mystics have long spoken of other planes of existence. These can be considered as *levels of perception* beyond the world of the physical senses.

Whatever word-symbols are used, all mean *degrees of awareness* in the process of transcending the illusion of a fractured Creation. Remember that illusion will seem to persist, even in the more "advanced" realms, until the *concept* of separateness is completely eliminated.

The purification of the heart-mind can help prevent having to repeat an earth experience! If the cleansing is comprehensive, it can eliminate having to experience the illusion of one or more other planes of existence.

Beloved brother-sisters, let us not procrastinate! Open the heart-mind to the guidance of Spirit. Apply the spiritual principles *now*, and change experience *here.* Each fearful thought and feeling released and dissolved brings closer the full experience of God.

In Heaven, the Real World, illusion does not exist. No need remains for separate means of identification, such as appearance or name. Energy fields are not seen as being separate. They function as One with the Life-Energy in the Mind of God. Until this state is experienced collectively by All Creation, there is still an apparent need for the correction of illusions.

As the heart-mind becomes increasingly filled with the radiance of universal Love, Peace and Joy, the awareness of the Christ-Self within consciousness expands... expands.... and expands. Less and less room remains for unwanted fear-based thoughts and feelings.

The physical body responds to increased awareness and we *feel* lighter—less bound by the heaviness of gravity. Every cell held captive in the illusion of form sparkles with the Light of the Life-Energy of the Source. *All this can happen here and now.*

When Spirit, or the God-Self, is consistently given direction over thoughts and feelings, the Light that surrounds and penetrates All becomes correspondingly more and more evident. The "etheric body" glows. This glow is often felt by others as divine Love whether or not it is seen.

You are a pure and shining Light, an *idea* in the Mind of God. This is your reality, your true identity. Here in this world of illusion you need to *think, feel and act like the Child of God.*

It may be helpful temporarily to *imagine* your divinity. With total surrender to Spirit and consistent practice of the divine principles, you naturally experience what you *already are in Truth*: the perfect Child of God.

This means that your thoughts, feelings and beliefs become totally radiant, loving, peaceful and joyful. Fear, guilt and resentment do not exist in the Mind of God, and they are not suitable emotions for any aspects of God's Creation. A pure heart-mind *reflects* the Heart-Mind of God. "Right" actions and joyous experience are *inevitable* when the heart-mind is a unified wellspring of Light, Love and Peace.

Daily prayer and meditation faithfully practiced with deep devotion and gratitude not only raise the vibrational rate, the power and amount of Light surrounding and interpenetrating the meditator is increased. The deeper spiritual awareness of Universal Love experienced through prayer and meditation is an open door to the Kingdom of Peace, the Power of Love and the Glory of Light—God's World.

Deep within the center of consciousness—perhaps just below the level of your awareness—is a truly innocent BEing, the gentle Child of God. It is the One that waits happily and patiently for your joyous awakening.

This is an ageless BEing that knows only the Light, Love, Peace and Joy of the Oneness of Life-Energy. It is a Child that has no knowledge of separateness. It does not fear anything because fear is unknown.

This holy Child is *You, the One God-Self.* Let It express Its Self through your self; be good friends with this BEing you love and that loves you with an eternal, ever present Love.

Let It be your playmate, your constant companion. Listen to the guidance of Its soft and gentle voice which will become increasingly easy to hear as you give It your *full attention.* Allow this Child to come nearer, closer to your heart. It *is* your heart. *It is the Love in you. It is your expression of God and All Creation.*

All Creation dances in pure joy! It sparkles and glows in constant ordered rhythm. No matter how it is *perceived,* whether in microcosmic or macrocosmic expression, all Life-Energy is in perpetual shining vibration, eternally unified with Its holy Source—God, the Creator of All-that-IS.

While concepts of space-time and form last, the macrocosm seems to move in stately progression and the microcosm appears to whirl with incredible rapidity. Still, the vibrations of All link in perfect harmony with God's Song of Creation.

As the expression of God, you are an inseparable part of this radiant timeless, formless, endless, joyful cosmic dance of Life, Light and Love *NOW*. This is the Peace of God.

So BE it!

O

M

A M E N

A

U

M

Appendix

The Lord's Prayer
(an interpretation)

Our Father-Mother GOD who is in Heaven, Source of
All-that-IS, holy is YOUR name ~ the name of Love.
YOUR Kingdom is here ~ It is everywhere; we need
only awareness of Its presence.
YOUR Will is done on earth as it is in Heaven ~ for
YOURS is the only Will; all else is
but wishes and wants.
YOU continually give us our daily bread ~ the unlimited
abundance of YOUR Life-Energy, the Thought of
YOUR Heart-Mind.
YOU forgive our mistakes as we forgive the mistakes
of others ~ for YOU see no error, nor can we who are
One with YOU.
We are not led into temptation when we remember that
YOU are our deliverance from the illusion of "evil."
For YOURS is the Kingdom of Peace, the Power of
Love, and the Glory of Light now and forever and ever
~ without end. Amen

Principles . . .

Affirmations ★ Prayers ★ Sayings

Thank You, God, for this perfect instant.

★ ★ ★

The Divine Mind of God is in charge of every aspect of any situation. All is well.

★ ★ ★

I *let* the God-Self within send out Its holy message of Love without interference.

★ ★ ★

I slander God's Creation whenever I see any part of It as imperfect.

★ ★ ★

In the Mind of God all is One and exists in perfect harmony. Thank You, God.

★ ★ ★

The only Real intimacy is in the total unity of God and All Creation.

The apparent distance of the "still, small voice" is not of space but of layers of consciousness—degrees of awareness.

★ ★ ★

In Love and forgiveness I recognize all aspects of Life—All Creation—as the One Child of God.

★ ★ ★

I am a child of Peace. God's Peace fills my heart-mind to overflowing. Thank You, God, for Peace.

★ ★ ★

Holy Spirit, help me to see the perfect God-nature, the I AM of everyone, everything, everywhere.

★ ★ ★

The God-Self, or Spirit, within is unaffected by any apparent malfunction of the body.

★ ★ ★

The Presence of God is *known* in the Mind we share.
The Presence of God is *felt* in the Heart we share.

As Spirit, I am without limits, wholly loving, peaceful and joyful. Thank You, God.

★ ★ ★

Every holy Thought that comes to mind is shared with All Creation.

★ ★ ★

I am an inseparable part of the Heart-Mind of God. Thank You, God, for Oneness!

★ ★ ★

God's Life-Energy, experienced as Light, Love, Peace and Joy, is *total* experience.

★ ★ ★

My holy shining reflection of God praises God. All Creation is in praise of God.

★ ★ ★

Nothing can be hurtful unless I give it the power to be so. My thoughts, feelings and beliefs determine what I experience on any level of perception.

The Mind of God is *where* I AM.

The Thought of God is *what* I AM.

★ ★ ★

STOP! I stop the activity of the superficial human-mind.

I allow what God IS to BE.

★ ★ ★

I cannot accept the *idea* of any kind of harm and still expect to be relieved of its seeming effects.

★ ★ ★

God's Mind knows only the singularity of the Whole.

★ ★ ★

The illusion of error is caused by thought that is misdirected and misapplied.

★ ★ ★

God universalizes; mortal man personalizes.

★ ★ ★

Peace needs the Light of Love and Joy to flourish.

Peace is not possible when fear and guilt are present.

The Universal Christ is seen in a pure mind and felt in a pure heart.

★ ★ ★

God's Will and Law are the harmonious, universally perfect and unified order of Creation.

★ ★ ★

God is the Source of all Life regardless of how it *appears* to manifest in the illusion.

★ ★ ★

NOW is a fresh, new instant lovingly, continually flowing from the Creative Mind of God.

★ ★ ★

Forgiveness, the open door to Divine Love, is the undoing of fear and guilt.

★ ★ ★

I am the holy Child of God whatever the appearance may *seem* to be. Nothing on any level of perception and activity can ever change this Truth.

God's Universal Love is my Blessing. Thank You, God.

★ ★ ★

Nothing I *do* can alter God's Love; Love can change how I *feel* and *think* — and *what I do.*

★ ★ ★

If I think about and discuss the apparent ills of the past, I ensure their repetition.

★ ★ ★

Everything I am exists in the Mind of God. I focus my thoughts on the Divine.

★ ★ ★

A mind that plans is anchored to the illusion of the material world. I let go—I am free—I trust God.

★ ★ ★

I am forever Spirit—unlimited, free and unassailable.

★ ★ ★

I am whole in mind, emotion and body. I remember the Love of God and the perfection of God's Creation.

I joyfully surrender my rational, human mind
to the Mind of God within. This is God's Will for me.

★ ★ ★

It is my Self, my holy Spirit, that I trust to remind me
about my identity.

★ ★ ★

I cannot avoid being what I *already* am, a spiritual
BEing of Light. I choose to recognize *Who I AM.*

★ ★ ★

A tired, confused and fearful humanity needs God's
Peace—extended through me.

★ ★ ★

Thank You, God, for Your gifts of Life-Energy, Light,
Love, Peace and Joy. I feel their presence within.

★ ★ ★

God is the Source of all Power. It can be used on behalf
of Love or to perpetuate fear, guilt and judgment.
The choice is mine to make.

God's Peace flows from one heart-mind to the next with feelings and thoughts of divine, forgiving non-judgmental Love.

★ ★ ★

The "illusion" cannot be analyzed, explained, judged nor understood because it is unreal and *does not exist!*

★ ★ ★

The Self, Universal Christ within, needs no healing. My concept of self does.

★ ★ ★

Healing of the body is an effect of healing the *mind.* A mind focused on health and wholeness is thinking in harmony with the Mind of God.

★ ★ ★

Divine Mind and Spirit are ONE; mortal mind and self are also one. With which do I choose to identify—- Truth or untruth?

Peace and Joy are integral parts of Divine Love; hence, Peace and Joy are integral parts of each other.

★ ★ ★

With help from Spirit within, I increase focus on the spiritual World and decrease focus upon the material world of appearances.

★ ★ ★

Worry is only another face of fear. The release is forgiveness, trust and unconditional Love.

★ ★ ★

In sparkling Light, Love and Joy is Peace freely, unconditionally given and received in an endless cycle encompassing All Creation.

★ ★ ★

I am thankful for forgiveness and Love that lead me gently, surely and safely along the Light-filled path.

★ ★ ★

All Creation is at Peace in the Mind of God.

Meditation Directions

1. Wear loose comfortable clothing; loosen the belt.
2. Make sure the body is relaxed; do some simple breathing and relaxation exercises if necessary.
3. Sit comfortably in a straight-backed chair with feet apart flat on the floor; or sit cross-legged in "lotus." If you lie down, you may fall asleep.
4. Close the eyes. Rest hands on thighs with palms turned up. Take three or four slow, deep breaths.
5. *Visualize and affirm being in and surrounded by a most brilliant white light.*
6. Mentally focus on a prayer or spiritual affirmation that has proved meaningful and helpful.
7. Quiet the active thoughts. *Wordlessly* open the heart-mind to receive the Peace of God.
8. *At the end of the period, reaffirm the presence of the white light and offer a prayer of thankfulness.*

Meditation Background Music

Listed below are a few of the many available cassette tapes suitable for accompanying silent meditation:

1. *Ascension To The All That Is* – Inner Harmony New Age Music by Robert Slap © 1987 Valley of the Sun Publishing
2. *Nocturne* – Emerald Web - Fortuna Records (BMI) © 1983 Bob Stohl and Kat Epple
3. *Petals* – Instrumental Visionary Music © 1981 Dreamweaver Music (BMI)
4. *Seapeace* – Music for Harp © 1978 Georgia Kelly
5. *Summer Rose* – Earthsong Productions 1983 Anne Williams
6. *Tibetan Bells,* Song of Silence – Geo-Imagery © 1989 Richard Klein

Some Sources for Further Reading and Study

A Course in Miracles

© Copyright 1975, Foundation for Inner Peace, Inc.
P. O. Box 1104
Glen Ellen, CA 95442

A Spiritual Philosophy for the New World

© Copyright 1990 by John Randolph Price
Publisher: Quartus Books
P. O. Box 1768
Boerne, TX 78006-6768

The Book of Knowledge: The Keys of Enoch

© Copyright 1977 by J. J. Hurtak
Publisher: The Academy for Future Science
P.O. Box FE
Los Gatos, CA 95030

The covers are from original symbolic paintings:

Front: *"Continual Creation,"* sub-titled *"Let there be Light—and there IS Light,"* 1985, acrylic, 48 x 48. The Creation of Life-Energy, seen as Light and felt as Love, is continuous and eternal.

Back: *"The self-Self,"* l993 acrylic, 26 x 26.
Light, visible evidence of the Life-Energy of the God-Self, interpenetrates and envelops the apparent density of the mortal "self."

Notes

Principles . . .

Principles . . .

Principles . . .